ENTREPRENEUR
GET YOUR ISH

SHATORA LADORNE

C.E.O. Rewired: Entrepreneur, Get Your Ish Together!

Copyright © 2025 Shatora Ladorne.

All rights reserved. In accordance with the U.S. Copyright Act of 1976, the scanning, uploading, and electronic sharing of any part of this book without permission of the publisher constitutes unlawful piracy and theft of the author's intellectual property. If you would like to use material from the book (other than for review purposes), prior written permission must be obtained by contacting the author at info@yourbusinessrewired.com.

ISBN: 978-1-951838-31-7

Legacy Builders Publishing
90daylegacybuilders.com

I dedicate this book:

To God— This assignment was Yours before it was ever mine. You entrusted me with something weighty, not to impress, but to impact. You didn't need a perfect vessel, just a willing one and when I hesitated, You reminded me who I am. When I felt defeated, You reminded me who You are.

To Jayceon and Ahmari — Every chapter, every decision, every pivot I've made has been with you in mind. You are my assignment. I write, build, and press forward to show you what's possible when you walk fully in who God created you to be.

My prayer is that you never settle, never play small, and never second-guess the power that's in you. Take up space. Make it count. Go after everything God put you on this earth to have, intentionally, with discipline, with wisdom, and with passion.

And To My Parents— I love you infinity + and to the Moon and back.

CONTENTS

Introduction: The Tables Always Turn i
Before You Begin

PHASE 1: THE TRUTH

Focus: Self-awareness, Honesty and Ownership

Chapter 1: Self-Assessment / Analysis ....…... 1
Chapter 2: Effective Communication 13
Chapter 3: Forecasting 25
Chapter 4: Consistency In Change ....…............. 38

PHASE 2: THE REWIRED

Focus: Alignment, Internal Leadership, Rewired Decision-Making Frameworks

Chapter 5: Faith + Business ....…... 51
Chapter 6: The Art of Course-Correcting 59
Chapter 7: When You Outgrow The Room 68

PHASE 3: THE EXPANSION

Focus: Execution, Visibility and Scalability

Chapter 8: CEO Energy ....…............ 78
Chapter 9: Rewired By Design 88
Chapter 10: What's Next ....….......... 99

COMPANION PDF

I personally don't like to write in my books. I like for them to look brand new in my library and ready for my legacy readers (grandchildren, great grandchildren and beyond) to enjoy the same as I did…

So don't forget to grab your **companion PDF** with the reflection prompts, tool breakdowns, and exercises to help you implement what you just read.

Whether you're a visual learner, a note-taker, or someone who needs that extra layer of accountability, this guide is built for you.

You can find it on the site as well at:

🔗**CEO Rewired Companion PDF**

https://rewiredcourses.com/companion-pdf

INTRODUCTION
THE TABLES ALWAYS TURN

Back when I was in high school, I was in a singing group and there was nothing I wanted more than to make it in music. It was me, my best friend, my cousin, and two other besties at the time. We were a bunch of kids with a dream and we were devoted. Every morning before class and every afternoon after school, we were outside practicing. On the phone singing. At each other's houses practicing. We wanted it badly.

Each scorching Texas afternoon after school, we rushed home to call all the major record labels on the West Coast, praying we would catch them before their lunchtime. Sony. Arista. Jive. Every day, we breathlessly gathered around the phone. We got to where we knew every receptionist at every major label by name.

One afternoon, a receptionist named Iesha picked up and said, "You know what? You call me every day. I'm going to patch you through. But don't tell anybody I did this."

Was this really happening? As the phone rang for what seemed like forever, we processed the fact that someone was about to make our dream come true. Whispers and humming to make sure we were on pitch immediately stopped when John Henry answered, "Hello?"

The second he answered, we didn't even say 'Hello' back. We just started singing.

He listened. He liked us. Then he stopped us. "Whoa, whoa, whoa. Okay, send me a demo. If I like it, I'll try to get you in on a couple of mini sessions."

We had two weeks! Two weeks. Fourteen days. 336 hours. All in all, there wasn't much time.

None of us had money for a studio, no connections, and I had already lied about my age to work at Pizza Hut, but my $90 paycheck wasn't enough. That left us with one choice- we recorded ourselves.

Early one morning before school, our graphic arts teacher, who had seen and heard us singing while wandering the halls, was kind enough to let us use the red room so that we wouldn't have background noise in our recording. Using a Talkgirl cassette recorder, we sang our hearts out. Then we wrapped the cassette tape in toilet paper, put it in a manila envelope, and slapped 16 stamps on it because we had no idea how many it took to get from Texas to California.

INTRODUCTION

A few weeks later, John called and said, "Either this is the most hilarious prank ever, or you guys got heart." We said, "We've got heart!"

So, he gave us a second chance. Another two weeks.

We begged our parents, scraped together the money, and finally got into a real studio. We were so excited that we got the demo made, but by the time we sent it in, it was a whole month too late. He never answered our calls again.

The group eventually broke up. I kept going with music for a while, but that moment has stuck with me throughout my life.

I have a tattoo on my chest as a reminder of that time. A cassette tape that is unraveling on the right, a turntable on the left and a heart in the center connecting the two. It represents my heart for my craft, my passion. Having the naivety to put myself out there and tenacity to pursue purpose, and the fact that even when things feel unraveled, the tables always turn.

This book is about that.

Because even when everything feels like it's coming undone, you still have the power to shift, to build, and to turn the tables in your favor. You don't wait for them to turn. You turn them yourself.

WHERE WE GO FROM HERE

That story? It wasn't just about a moment. It was a mirror. A reflection that forced me to stop and ask hard questions. Not just about the situation, but about me.

And that's exactly where we're starting.

Because building and leading a business is about much more than just strategy. It's about alignment. Before you can lead a company well, you've got to lead yourself through your own mess, mindset, patterns, and pivots.

This book is broken into **three phases**, each one designed to walk you through a critical part of becoming the kind of entrepreneur who has hustle, is healing, makes the tough decisions, leads, and expands with sniper focus.

PHASE I: THE TRUTH

You can't rewire what you're not willing to see. This phase is about honesty. It's about looking at where things really stand in your thinking, your communication, your forecasting, your decisions and calling it what it is. No fluff. No filters. Just truth.

PHASE II: THE REWIRED

This is where we break patterns and rebuild foundations. In this phase, you'll learn how to progress with consistency, course correct with intention, and lead with faith and strategy, even when things get uncomfortable.

PHASE III: THE EXPANSION

Now we build. From overflow, not overwork. From alignment, not anxiety. This phase helps you step into CEO level energy, legacy level thinking, and vision backed execution that actually matches your lifestyle.

BEFORE YOU BEGIN

As a business strategist I specialize in guiding people through high stakes transitions like launching a new venture or scaling an existing one. My sweet spot? Working with entrepreneurs in emerging industries, particularly those who value community impact, personal growth, and strategic planning. I help bold ideas become real, actionable roadmaps.

So, understand this: this book is a blueprint.

A guide. A toolbox. A conversation. A companion for the days when business is booming and especially for the days when everything feels like it's falling apart.

You'll find frameworks and tools throughout these pages, but let me be clear, this isn't theory. These are lived-in, field-tested truths from the real business trenches.

I didn't build a business off buzzwords. I built it on depth, alignment, and action. Everything in this book is built to meet you where you are, whether you're just getting started or managing a multi-million-dollar machine that no longer feels like yours.

You won't find stiff corporate case studies or one-size-fits-all formulas. You'll find tools you can grab mid-crisis, in the middle of a launch gone sideways, or right before that late-night decision that could shift everything. Tools you can actually use when ish gets real.

INTRODUCTION

What's in these pages is my Rewired Framework™. A God given framework that applies far beyond business. It's a framework you can come back to in every area of your life.

So, keep it close. Write in it. Tag the pages. Drop it on your desk when you're mapping out your next venture. This book belongs to you now.

Let's rewire, not just once, but as many times as it takes.

PHASE I
THE TRUTH

FOCUS:

SELF-AWARENESS

HONESTY

OWNERSHIP

CHAPTER ONE

SELF-ASSESSMENT / ANALYSIS

This is where everything starts.

You cannot grow into the leader, the business owner, the parent, the partner, or the person you're called to be if you're not willing to be honest about where you are now.

Self-assessment requires awareness. You have to be able to say, "Here's what's working. Here's what's not. Here's what needs to shift."

That level of honesty can sting. Especially when you realize the biggest barrier isn't external, it's you.

But awareness is power. And until you can sit with the truth, you'll stay stuck in cycles you were meant to outgrow.

Let me give you an example.

In football, whenever a team gains a first down, they move the marker, or the chains, to signify progress. For years, I watched the chains move. My sweat and energy poured into the work I did and the company I worked for. I remember being promised a promotion. I showed up. I led. I trained people who eventually got roles I had been asking for—roles that were promised to me by leaders who have moved on. Every time I was told, "Your time is coming." And I believed them.

So, in faith, I planned for it.

I made moves based on that promise. Financial ones, mental ones, emotional ones. I made changes in my life, trusting those commitments. And I consistently watched the chains move.

Then, it happened. Several other people got promoted. Again, not me. So, here's what I did, and how I reacted to those promises being broken. I smiled. I congratulated them. I nodded like it didn't rock me. I watched the chains move.

Even in the next one-on-one with my manager, they asked, "How are you?"

"I'm fine," I said, ignoring the shakiness in my voice.

But when I logged off that call, I sat in silence until I exploded in frustration, "I'm not fine! I'm pissed!"

I had mapped out what that raise would cover. I had plans for that money. But they never guaranteed the money. I had built a plan on the assumption that someone else would follow through.

A mentor of mine once said, "You can't count your money in other people's pockets."

Whew! That part.

Here's the lesson: What someone else did or didn't give you doesn't define your value. But their decision gives you data, and you need to use it.

An area to assess:

Where are your expectations placed?

How much of your plan is built on someone else's word?

What financial or mental shifts have you made before you had real confirmation?

Rewiring stings when it starts.

It starts with acknowledging what's real. You don't have to lie to yourself just to keep the peace. You don't have to internalize disappointment and call it "patience." Nor do you have to keep hoping for something that keeps showing you it's obviously not coming.

Self-assessment is how you reclaim your power.

Let's bring this even closer to home.

There was a time in my life where I realized I was holding onto a version of myself that no longer fit. I kept doing things I had outgrown. Saying yes to things that drained me. I was entertaining relationships that no longer aligned with where I was going. The truth was, I wasn't stuck or scared. I was comfortable. Too comfortable to let go of what was familiar and too stubborn in the thought that changing course would look like quitting.

It took one moment, one honest conversation with myself to shift it.

I asked: "What am I holding onto that's holding me back?"

The answer came quickly and it wasn't just one thing. It was a list. A list of habits, routines, thoughts, and people I had never "audited." I just kept living with them and that's when I realized:

Self-assessment isn't about fixing everything. It's about facing everything.

You don't need all the answers to make a change. You just need to stop pretending everything is fine when you know it isn't.

SELF-ASSESSMENT / ANALYSIS

HOW TO START YOUR OWN ASSESSMENT

You don't need a five-step formula to reflect on your life, your leadership, or your business.

Just give yourself the honesty and the space.

Here's a few simple questions I have my clients ask themselves when they feel stuck but don't know where to start:

THE REWIRED CHECK-IN

1. **What feels heavy right now?** Where are you holding stress, tension, or confusion?

_____
_____
_____
_____
_____
_____
_____
_____
_____

2. **What's no longer aligned?** Look at your habits, relationships, work, and environment. What's taking more than it's giving?

_____
_____
_____
_____
_____
_____
_____
_____
_____

SELF-ASSESSMENT / ANALYSIS

3. **Why do I keep avoiding the obvious?** What conversation, decision, or shift have you pushed to the side and find out why?

_____
_____
_____
_____
_____
_____
_____
_____
_____

Use these questions to clear out the mental noise. Write the answers. Let them lead you to clarity.

YOUR TURN

What have you continued to hope for even though the pattern shows you it's not coming?

_____
_____
_____
_____
_____
_____
_____

Where have you handed over your power, hoping someone else would "fix it" or "get it right" this time?

_____
_____
_____
_____
_____
_____
_____

What truth do you already know that you've been trying to avoid?

_____
_____
_____
_____
_____
_____
_____

SELF-ASSESSMENT / ANALYSIS

What needs to shift before you start blaming others for what you keep accepting?

_____
_____
_____
_____
_____
_____

**Write it. Reflect on it. Be honest enough to name it.
Then prepare to move forward with that truth in hand.**

REWIRED IN REAL LIFE

There was someone I cared about deeply. We shared a special connection, showed up for each other and we both genuinely meant well, but it became clear we were wired very differently.

I valued daily connection, simple check-ins, intentional presence, and a steady rhythm of communication. Not out of neediness, but out of care. A quick "Hey, you good?" once a day was enough. They said they wanted the same thing, and for a while I believed we were aligned. But were we really on the same wavelength?

I came to realize that while we both longed to feel cared for in the same way, we didn't know how to give in the same way. I showed up with consistency, quick check-ins, and clear words, but those things didn't register as necessary to them. What felt natural and meaningful to me never crossed their mind as something to offer back. It wasn't intentional or cruel, it was simply unfamiliar. They had never been expected to give that kind of presence, so it didn't come naturally.

They felt frustrated by the things I expected. What took time to surface was that unmet, unspoken expectations in our relationship had caused fractures in the foundation. Their unmet needs were mirroring mine, and I kept trying to pull emotional connection and understanding from someone who just honestly didn't have it to offer.

That's when I had to pause.

SELF-ASSESSMENT / ANALYSIS

This was a personal moment of self-assessment. I knew they didn't have the emotional vocabulary, the experience, or even the awareness for what I was asking. And if I *knew* that, then it wasn't fair to keep blaming them for not being able to give me something they never received themselves.

So, I had to ask myself: *What am I doing here?* Am I choosing to stay in a dynamic that will always feel uneven? Or can I accept the limitations and realign how I show up?

That's the heart of mature self-assessment... and yes sometimes it sucks!

Whether it's a friend, a partner, a parent, or a client, if someone can't meet you where you are, it's not your job to drag them there. It's your job to decide:

Is this connection for a reason, a season, or is this just something I'm still choosing?

Self-assessment begins by telling the truth about what's in front of you and then deciding what you're going to do with it.

CLARITY REWIRED

When you're sitting in frustration, disappointment, or even confusion, ask yourself:

1. Am I trying to get something from someone who doesn't have it to give?

2. What would change if I accepted that and made decisions from that truth instead of that hope?

3. Is this relationship seasonal, situational, or something I'm choosing to sustain?

Clarity means you stop begging people to become someone they've never been. You then start deciding how you want to move based on who they already are.

CHAPTER TWO

EFFECTIVE COMMUNICATION

Communication can be your greatest asset or the very thing that burns the house down with you in it.

It's not just about what you say. It's about when you say it, how you say it, why you're saying it, and who you're saying it to. Some of the most important communication doesn't come out of your mouth at all, it comes through silence, body language, and your ability to listen.

I used to struggle with knowing when to speak up. I'd be in a room, either at work or in an entrepreneurial setting when an intense conversation would be happening. I'd listen, process, and have a strategic solution way before it was ever said out loud. Because I'm a teacher at heart, my brain naturally breaks things down. I could hear the problem, see the gap, and spot the system needed to fix it, and fast!

But I wouldn't speak.

It was never because I didn't know what to say, but because I convinced myself someone else in the room had to have already thought of it. Or that they'd say it better. Or that it wasn't my place.

Then, no more than ten or fifteen minutes later, someone else would say exactly what I was thinking. Everyone would nod in agreement. Those moments made me cringe, because I knew I could've added value earlier… if I had just opened my mouth.

There's this popular phrase: "You should never be the smartest person in the room." But I want to expand on that. Yes, make sure you're in rooms where you can grow. But just because you're not the smartest doesn't mean you have nothing to offer. Don't shrink. Don't silence yourself under the assumption that someone else is more qualified or the idea that the value has already been spoken.

Bring your brilliance to the room. Even if it echoes what someone else has already said. Your voice has weight. Your delivery might be the one that makes it finally click.

But just like there's a time to speak up, there's also a time to shut up!

Yes, I said it.

There's wisdom that comes from knowing when to hold it in. When your emotions are high. Your jaw is clenching. When you're more reactive than reflective.

You don't always have to "check" someone. You don't always have to set the record straight. Sometimes, you just need to come to an understanding. A pause doesn't mean you're weak. It means you care about how your words land and you respect what's on the line enough to wait until you can speak with clarity instead of giving a piece of your mind. When communication is done right, it builds trust, creates safety and it unlocks opportunity.

It works cross-functionally—at home, in business, in all of our relationships and in leadership.

WHERE COMMUNICATION GOES WRONG

Have you ever had someone say, "If you weren't sure, why didn't you ask?" The kicker is, you were sure! You thought you followed the instructions exactly as given, or did precisely what was asked of you. So, why would you go back and ask for clarification on something you were confident about? You don't know what you don't know, especially when it's all in someone else's mind.

We don't usually mean to communicate poorly, but it happens when we're tired, overwhelmed, unsure, or triggered. The most common breakdown in communication that I see in my clients, teams, relationships and businesses sound like this:

"They should know what I meant."

"I didn't want to come off too harsh."

"I figured if it was that important, they'd ask or ask again."

"It wasn't the right time, so I just let it go."

Here's where it breaks down:

Letting things go feels easier in the moment, but over time it creates confusion, distance, or even resentment. The message never lands, the need goes undiscovered, and people are left guessing what went wrong.

Even when you say nothing, you're still saying something.

Avoiding a conversation doesn't erase the issue, it just delays the impact.

Here is a tip:

There's a difference between silence and self-control. Silence avoids clarity. Self-control waits for the right words with the right weight.

That's emotional intelligence in communication at its finest.

Not holding it in or blowing up, but pausing with purpose, so that when you speak, you're leading the outcome... not just reacting to the moment.

COMMUNICATION IN LEADERSHIP

Whether you're running a team or navigating client relationships, the way you communicate sets the tone for how others show up.

If you're vague, people will hesitate.

If you're always intense, people will walk on eggshells.

If you're avoidant, people will fill in the blanks and usually with the worst-case scenario.

On the flip side:

Clear leaders earn trust faster.

Thoughtful communicators gain loyalty.

Direct but respectful feedback accelerates performance.

One of the biggest myths in leadership is that your title earns you communication privileges. It doesn't. Presence, Respect, Clarity. Those are the essentials

YOUR TURN

What conversations have you held back from out of fear or self-doubt?

_____
_____
_____
_____
_____
_____
_____
_____

Have you ever spoken too soon and caused more damage than progress?

_____
_____
_____
_____
_____
_____
_____
_____

What's one conversation you need to have with clarity and courage this week?

_____
_____
_____
_____
_____
_____
_____
_____

What's one you need to pause before having?

_____
_____
_____
_____
_____
_____
_____
_____

Write it. Reflect on it. Then move with intention.

REWIRED IN REAL LIFE

Let's talk about the fine line between silence and sabotage.

My friend, Jordan and I naturally formed a business partnership. Together, we saw so much potential to impact the world. We actively collaborated our businesses together, providing strategic advice and sharing ideas. The energy was there. The vision was there. Together, we were making moves, and it felt right.

Then it happened.

Jordan launched an amazing concept, which we had been working on together from the ground up. I had provided intricate details and spent time pouring into this. We had planted this seed together. But instead of a joint celebration of our achievement, it was a huge letdown, as I was excluded. No credit. No conversation. Just a rollout.

And at that moment, I had a choice.

My ego begged me to go on the attack, call Jordan out and cut ties. Wisdom called for me to pause and communicate from a grounded place. It took everything in me not to lead with ego. Instead, I asked myself: What conversation *needs* to happen here that still honors me and keeps me aligned with how I want to show up?

So, I had the conversation. Calmly. Firmly. Directly. I shared my perspective and how it felt, and I made space for whatever was to come of it.

We didn't end on bad terms, but the raw honesty helped me realign how I interact and partner with them.

In business, and in life, clear communication protects your peace. It draws lines without burning bridges and it teaches people how to treat you. You get the real time feedback you need to move forward.

Power doesn't often come from your volume; it comes from clear communication.

Now on the flip side, let's talk personally.

Have you ever been in a relationship (romantic or family) where something simple blew up because both people just shut down?

You assumed they knew what you needed.

They assumed you were okay.

Nobody said anything.

Now you're both looking at each other sideways, harboring frustration over an issue that could've been solved with an adult conversation.

You're arguing about dishes when it's really about feeling unsupported. You're talking about tone when it's really about timing. You're being passive-aggressive because deep down you don't feel safe saying what's real.

That's not communication. That's emotional warfare.

The truth is, most people don't know how to communicate until it's too late. They wait until they're boiling, ready to explode and their body language is saying everything their mouth won't.

Emotional intelligence requires self-regulation. That means you've got to know when to speak and when to pause, not to punish, but to process.

When your communication is off, your connections suffer, so does your clarity in your business as well.

When your communication is healthy, direct, built on respect, you don't just talk better, you live better.

CLARITY REWIRED

Use this before any difficult or important conversation—whether it's with a client, team member, partner, or friend:

1. What do I ACTUALLY want to communicate?

2. What impact do I want my words to have?

3. Am I speaking to solve, to be heard, or to be right?

These questions don't soften the truth. They sharpen it.

CHAPTER THREE

FORECASTING

Ever had that season where you said yes to things that you knew would be too much at the time and would absolutely have you overextended, but you said it anyway?

You know those times… Another unpaid speaking engagement that's taking away from revenue generating activity, another after hours call with a client, or another last minute meet-up with the boys (or the girls) where you agreed even though you were already exhausted.

And then what happened?

You didn't show up as your best self because you were stretched way too thin.

Your body was tired and you were falling asleep at dinner. Your mind was overloaded about business, now you're questioning yourself and are unsure if you were failing or if you just aren't cut out for this entrepreneur life.

If you're going to grow or lead a business well, you have to stop playing catch-up. Forecasting helps you build a plan based on your actual capacity beyond your ambition.

I've seen countless business owners start the week already behind. They're booked, busy, and overwhelmed. Everything is urgent. They're responding to the day instead of leading the business.

Don't worry, I've been there too.

You don't have to say yes just to prove something. You don't have to keep going just because you're used to being the one who gets it done.

You're allowed to pause and project. You're allowed to lead from a place of peace, not panic.

WHAT FORECASTING ACTUALLY MEANS

Forecasting means you ask:

"If I take this on, what's going to get neglected?"

"If I say yes, what am I silently saying no to?"

"If I don't slow down now, what's going to break later?"

Forecasting is the discipline of deciding in advance who gets access to you and on what terms.

It's looking at your time, your energy, your responsibilities, and your business patterns, and building structure around them.

When you're scheduling tasks, you're actually protecting your energy, making space to lead, and avoiding burnout that can be prevented with better planning.

When you forecast well, you stop overcommitting. You plan your time, your output, and your recovery with intention. You lead instead of scramble.

A SEASON I GOT IT WRONG

There was a period of time where everything felt like momentum. My name was circulating in rooms I hadn't even entered. New clients were coming in. I was booked to speak out across the country. I had a full calendar of projects, meetings, events and I still said yes to more.

On paper, it looked like progress. In reality, I was past my limits.

One day the most horrific thing happened, I sat down for a call with a new, very high ticket client and can you guess what happened? I completely blanked. I couldn't remember where we left off. My notes didn't help. I was there physically, but not mentally. I didn't feel like myself, and I knew it.

That was my wake-up call. I had built a schedule that didn't protect my values or my execution. There was no margin for error. No buffer. No space to reset or think.

From that point on, I started planning differently. I didn't stop building, but I made sure what I was building could support the pace that I was moving.

FORECASTING GOES BEYOND TIME

Your calendar only tells part of the story. Lead your business with a sniper's focus by forecasting across every part of the operation. That means planning your time, your money, your team, your energy, and your audience.

Forecasting Your Money

Don't just track income. Study your financial patterns. Look at your slow seasons, your peak months, your payment timelines, and your upcoming expenses. If you know revenue slows down in the summer, build a cash cushion in the spring. If your biggest vendor payment hits every 90 days, stagger your other large investments so they don't land in the same week.

Build your money forecast around reality, not your best month. Set money aside for taxes, renewals, and upgrades *before* they sneak up. Create a baseline of what it costs to run your business each month so you know when you're truly profitable, not just busy.

Tip: Use an accounting system or a simple spreadsheet to track recurring expenses, high-cost seasons, and revenue cycles. Review it monthly and make decisions from that...

Forecasting Your Team

If you're managing people (or plan to), you need to think beyond who's hired and who's paid. Forecasting your team means knowing what skills you'll need in the next season of business and what kind of leadership you'll have to bring to support it.

Don't wait until you're underwater to hire. Identify your bottlenecks now and decide if it's a system or a staffing issue. Build a 30–60–90-day plan for each role so onboarding doesn't feel like guesswork.

Anticipate time off, peak project windows, and emotional load. Good teams burn out when the business keeps changing but the structure doesn't.

Tip: Every quarter, review how long tasks are taking, what keeps slipping through the cracks, and where communication is stalling. That's where your next hire or restructure needs to happen.

Forecasting Your Energy

You know when you're most focused. You also know when your body starts slowing down, even when you ignore it. Start building your calendar around those patterns instead of pushing through them.

If your energy dips midweek, don't schedule calls on Wednesdays. If creative work is easier in the morning, block off that time instead of filling it with admin. Build in recovery before you feel fried. You'll perform better and stay sharper longer.

Tip: Use color-coded blocks on your calendar to highlight high-energy, mid-energy, and low-energy times. Match your tasks accordingly. Make recovery a standing appointment and not a last resort.

Forecasting Your Market

Don't post and pray. Haha… Let me rephrase that. Don't launch without warming up your audience. Forecasting your market means paying attention to what they respond to, when they show up, and what they're actually asking for.

Study your engagement trends. Listen to what clients are struggling with right now. Pay attention to industry shifts. This will help you align your messaging, offers, and timing with real demand outside of your own goals.

Tip: Use a content or offer calendar that aligns with both your business rhythm and your audience's behavior. Make space to gather feedback before you make your next move.

WHY MOST PEOPLE SKIP THIS

People usually skip forecasting when things are going well. They're busy, so they assume the system is working. But if you're too busy to think ahead, you're building your business on hope and adrenaline. That's also how you end up resenting the very thing you've risked everything for.

The right time to forecast is BEFORE things get messy. That's when you have the space to adjust. That's when you make better decisions. That's how you even protect yourself from YOU!

YOUR TURN

Where do you keep running out of time, even though the warning signs are there?

_____
_____
_____
_____
_____
_____

What have you agreed to that didn't match your actual capacity?

_____
_____
_____
_____
_____
_____

What would become easier if you looked 30 to 60 days ahead instead of just reacting?

_____
_____
_____
_____
_____
_____
_____
_____

What area of your life or business needs more structure before it becomes a problem?

_____
_____
_____
_____
_____
_____
_____

Write it. Anticipate it. Then move like you've already seen what's coming.

REWIRED IN REAL LIFE

Marcus ran a successful residential renovation company. Revenue was steady, referrals were solid, and he had a mix of employees and subcontractors helping him stay on track. From the outside, business was booming. But behind the scenes, Marcus was winging it—and it was starting to catch up with him.

He decided to expand into a second market. The opportunity made sense on paper. More visibility, higher-paying clients, and the kind of growth that looks great in a quarterly review. But once we sat down to map it all out, the cracks became obvious.

His onboarding process was still manual. Every new client needed a custom welcome email, back-and-forth scheduling, and scattered reminders—none of it automated. His content hadn't been updated in months, so the messaging on his website and social media spoke to where the business used to be, not where it was going.

His team was loyal, but they were over it. They were one more "mandatory overtime" text away from walking out and leaving him a solo act again. They cared about the business but didn't see a plan.

We paused the expansion and went into forecasting mode.

What systems would break if we added more volume? What support did the team need now, not six months from now?

What messaging needed to evolve to attract the right kind of clients in this new market?

We built out an automated onboarding workflow of emails, intake forms, and next steps, so the team didn't have to personally chase every new lead. We standardized the follow-up process so no client slipped through the cracks. Then we realigned the offers, cleaned up the copy, and rebuilt the website to reflect the results his clients were actually getting now.

Internally, we held a Team Rewired Clarity Session. Roles were updated. Expectations were set. Deliverables were assigned. No more guesswork.

Only after that foundation was stable did we revisit the expansion strategy. This time, we started with research, pre-launch content, and interest list building. When the doors opened, his systems didn't buckle under pressure. His team wasn't overwhelmed. The launch was clean and sustainable.

That's the power of forecasting. It doesn't just make growth easier. It makes everything you've already built better.

CLARITY REWIRED

Use this before your next launch, pivot, or planning season.

1. **What am I already carrying that hasn't been scheduled or supported?** Don't ignore the hidden pressure. If it takes energy, it counts.

2. **What's coming up that will require more time, focus, or money than I've planned for?** Be honest. Build space around it now, not later.

3. **What support or systems do I need in place to do this well?** Think: people, process, tools, and boundaries.

Forecasting doesn't have to be complicated. It just has to be done.

Spot the pattern. Plot your pivot.

CHAPTER FOUR

CONSISTENCY IN CHANGE

BEFORE THE STORY: WHY THIS MATTERS

Every entrepreneur reaches a growth spurt, where everything changes, your schedule, your priorities, your team, your client base. What worked last quarter suddenly feels outdated. What felt like flow now feels like friction. You look around and realize the game didn't change... the conditions did.

That's when consistency gets tested.

This chapter dives into forcing yourself out of the same routine season after season. We'll talk about understanding how true consistency isn't rigid, it's responsive. Your systems, your habits, and your leadership should be built to hold steady *and* adjust. That's where the strength is, not in how tightly you hold on, but in how well you adapt without losing your center.

OH WHAT A DAY AT CHICK-FIL-A

I couldn't wait to tell you the story about my day at Chick-fil-A.

Not because of the chicken, but because of the consistency. Right after COVID-19, when things started opening back up, I went to a Chick-fil-A to pick up my food. Instead of going through the drive-thru, I went inside.

Now, if you've ever been inside a Chick-fil-A, you know what to expect: warm greetings, multiple team members smiling at you the moment you walk in, and a level of efficiency that almost feels like a dance. But that day? Silence. There were at least a dozen employees behind the counter, doing their jobs, fulfilling orders, staying busy, but no one greeted me. No "hello," no "welcome in," no acknowledgment.

And I froze.

I checked the sign above me to make sure I was standing in the right place. I looked at my phone to make sure my order had gone through. I was literally checking myself to see what I had done wrong.

Eventually, one of the workers acknowledged me, handed me my order and sent me on my way with the "my pleasure" that I was accustomed to.

I made my way back to my car and then it hit me.

I wasn't actually checking myself in the restaurant because I had done anything wrong. I was checking myself because they had been so consistent for so long, that the moment something was off, I assumed I was the problem.
That's the power of consistency.

When a brand, or a person shows up in excellence over and over again, people begin to trust not just the product, but the presence.

Chick-fil-A could start selling chicken pizza or chicken tacos tomorrow and the line would probably still be wrapped around the building. Why? Because their systems and their standards are strong enough to support the change.

Change is inevitable. If your current situation can't handle change, then your business, your relationships and your teams will fall apart the second something unexpected happens.

Here's the two-fold truth:
1. **Your systems must be strong enough to adapt.** Whether it's business, family, or personal growth, life will throw something at you that requires a disruption and when that disruption happens, the question becomes: are your systems strong enough to

carry despite the change, or will everything crumble because the process was too fragile?

2. **Your brand must be trustworthy enough to handle disruption.** I don't mean the external brand—the visuals, the logo, the color palette. I'm talking about the brand of YOU. Are you the type of person that when things don't go as planned, people can still trust you'll make it right? Can your integrity be counted on when the outcome isn't certain?

Consistency without adaptability is rigidity. Change without consistency is chaos.

Consistency with change? That's leadership.

You don't just need a standard. You need a standard that can stretch. That means you're consistent enough to be trusted, and flexible enough to be useful.

Sometimes we fall off in our personal or professional lives, and we think, "Oh, I'll get back on track eventually." But that slow fade? It's dangerous. Just like excellence is noticed when it's maintained, its absence is noticed even more.

Consistency is showing up in excellence over and over. Being intentional about how you show up, even when the conditions change.

This is where you rewire your discipline.

LET'S GET PERSONAL

Maybe for you, it's not Chick-fil-A. Maybe it's your morning routine—or what used to be your morning routine. There was a time you meditated, journaled, drank water, hit the gym. You felt good. Clear. Focused.

Then life got busy. Travel picked up. Clients increased. You can't remember the last time you even entertained the thought of a date. And now it's been six months and you don't even recognize your rhythm.

But here's the real question: did the circumstances throw you off, or did you stop showing up for *you*?

We talk a lot about building brands people can count on. But can you count on *yourself*?

Can you trust you'll follow through on what you said you'd do even if no one's watching?

Can your own habits count on you?

It's easy to build consistency when everything's stable. The real test is: can you maintain that same level of excellence when things shift?

That's what separates those who are simply motivated from those who are truly wired to lead.

HOW TO BUILD CONSISTENCY THAT CAN HOLD CHANGE

Consistency doesn't mean you do everything the same way forever. It means you commit to a standard then you protect that standard even when the circumstances shift.

If your systems only work when everything is perfect, you don't have systems, you have wishes.

Here's what consistency looks like in real life:

1. **Use systems that reflect how you actually move.**
   If your planner has 50 boxes but your brain works in top-3 priorities, simplify. Don't copy someone else's system because it looks clean online. Build what works for your attention span, your lifestyle, and your business model.

2. **Build checkpoints into your habits.**
   Set a recurring day or time to review what's still working. Weekly check-ins with yourself or your team. End-of-day wrap-ups. Monthly rhythm reviews. These don't have to be long, but they help you course-correct before things unravel.

3. **Protect your core routines when things shift.**
   Pick 2–3 "non-negotiables" that keep you grounded. That might be a morning walk, a Friday CEO meeting, or an end-of-day power-down. Even in chaos, these anchors keep you connected to who you are and how you lead.

4. **Don't confuse tight routines with strong leadership.**
   Flexibility is not failure. There will be days where your structure breaks. The strength is in your ability to return, not to the schedule, but to the *standard*. Come back with intention, not punishment.

YOUR TURN

Where have you started to let your standard slip, personally or professionally?

_____
_____
_____
_____
_____
_____

Are your systems built to evolve, or are they built so tight that one shift throws everything off?

_____
_____
_____
_____
_____
_____

What do people expect from you, and are you still delivering that level of consistency?

_____
_____
_____
_____
_____
_____

Consistency is what builds the brand. Change is what reveals the strength of it. Let's rewire both.

CLARITY REWIRED

Use this to stay rooted when everything around you is shifting.

1. **What's my real baseline—what are the habits, routines, or standards that keep me grounded when things feel off?**
   Think about what pulls you out of the fog. Not just what looks good, but what works.

2. **What part of my current routine or system is no longer serving me—but I'm still holding onto it?**
   This is your permission to adjust.

3. **What one commitment can I make to myself this week that reflects the consistency I want to return to?**
   Make it doable. Make it true. Then protect it.

REWIRED IN REAL LIFE

Let's talk about that internal conversation. Yes, that one that you don't post about.

You promised yourself you'd get serious. You swore this would be the year you stayed consistent. You even mapped out your schedule, color-coded your calendar, and gave it a cute name like "Discipline December" or "Millionaire Morning Routine."

And then... life.

One late night turned into a week of bad sleep. One client crisis pulled your focus. The gym stopped seeing you. The meal prep turned into Uber Eats. The journaling turned into reacting to DMs.

And now you're staring at your screen wondering, *"How did I get off track again?"*

But here's the truth: falling off doesn't make you a failure. It makes you human.

What matters is whether you let the fall become your foundation, or your bounce back.

Consistency in real life doesn't mean perfection. It means your comeback rate gets quicker, your awareness is sharper and you recognize when things are slipping *before* they spiral.

The goal isn't to overhaul everything every time life changes; it's to build tools that evolve with you.

When something stops working? Rewire it. Unplug it from the place that's no longer serving and plug it into what will.

PHASE II
THE REWIRED

FOCUS:

ALIGNMENT

INTERNAL LEADERSHIP

REWIRED DECISION-MAKING FRAMEWORKS

We're not just building for the sake of success. We're building from alignment.

In this next phase, strategy alone isn't enough. We have to dig deeper.

This is where your decision-making sharpens. Peace becomes part of the plan and purpose. Apply a little pressure that drives the vision.

If faith is part of your foundation, then it should show up in how you build. Not just in how you pray over the outcome, but how you walk through the process. Because when the stakes rise, and the noise grows louder, what you believe will shape what you build.

CHAPTER FIVE

FAITH + BUSINESS

Faith and business don't belong in separate corners.

For those of us who lead from a calling beyond ambition, faith goes far beyond a footnote, it's the framework. It shapes how we make decisions, how we recover, and how we lead in every area of life.

This chapter is about that alignment. I'm not talking religion. Not talking rituals. But real, faith-led strategy that holds weight when logic runs out.

I've always kept God at the center of how I operate.

Not in a "Sunday morning, post-a-scripture" kind of way. But in a this-decision-needs-prayer, this-client-needs-discernment, this-deal-needs-alignment kind of way.

Faith in business doesn't allow you to avoid risk. Your risks are rooted in something deeper than ego.

Because entrepreneurship will test everything you believe.

It will test your confidence.

It will test your character.

It will test your consistency.

And it will definitely test your faith.

DISCLAIMER

Faith doesn't guarantee that you'll feel qualified.

I've walked into rooms where I felt completely out of place. I was the quietest. The newest. The one with the least connections. The one without the Ivy League background. The one with a past.

And I still showed up!

If God gave me a seat at the table, I wasn't about to talk myself out of it.

The difference between being invited and being assigned is that one is about optics and the other is about obedience. When you've been assigned by God to operate in a space, no title, no degree, and no human validation can compete with the anointing that follows your faith.

Your faith that gets you in the room, but your obedience that keeps you there.

Faith + Business requires launching scared. Walking away from deals that look good but don't feel right. Saying no when your bank account is saying please God yes!

It's trusting that purpose won't let you drown, even when profit takes a dip.

Some of the most powerful moves I've made came from prayer, not a pitch deck. There were situations when strategy couldn't save me, only faith.

Praying over decisions before signing the dotted line.

Trusting that what God gave me wasn't just a good idea, it was a God idea.

It was knowing when to pause and when to press. When to sit still, and when to speak up.

You'll know you're moving in alignment when:
- Peace follows your yes, even when people don't understand it.

- Conviction pulls you back, even when everything looks like it all adds up.

- Provision shows up just in time, after you've leapt without the net.

Faith + Business is God's perfect positioning. You have to walk out your calling knowing that you were assigned and when it gets hard, and it will, you don't hustle harder. You hear clearer.

YOUR TURN

Where have you been trying to force what should be faith-led?

_____
_____
_____
_____
_____
_____

What decision are you facing that needs prayer, not pressure?

_____
_____
_____
_____
_____
_____

Are you running your business with God, or just hoping He blesses what you're already doing?

_____
_____
_____
_____
_____
_____

Pause. Pray. Listen. Then carry on in peace.

FAITH CHECK

Use this when you're unsure if a decision is spirit-led or pressure-driven, especially when the opportunity looks good, but something feels off.

1. **Is this aligned with what I asked for—or just what showed up first?**
   Just because it's available doesn't mean it's aligned.

2. **Am I moving because of peace—or because of pressure?**
   Discernment doesn't rush. Faith can move fast, but it never forces.

3. **If this completely fell apart tomorrow, would I still believe it was the right move today?**
   Obedience won't always feel easy. But it will feel right.

You don't need a perfect plan to move forward, but if you're going to trust anything, trust the peace that comes from faith.

REWIRED IN REAL LIFE

A while back, I was preparing to launch a full-scale leadership and personal development program under my Rewired brand. It was supposed to be the next big expansion. A program that brought together everything I had taught in parts, now wrapped into one transformational experience.

I had mapped out the curriculum, talked to partners and lined up the strategy. Everything looked aligned on the surface.

I just couldn't shake the feeling that something wasn't right. It wasn't fear. It wasn't sabotage. It was that still, quiet beckoning I've come to recognize over time. The one that tells me to wait, even when everything "makes sense."

So, I asked.

Straight up: "God, if this is not what you want me building right now—shut it down."

I get to laugh in hindsight because for whatever reason I was surprised that He did it. He shut it down.

Not dramatically. But deliberately. The people I was going to collaborate with started pulling back. The timeline started shifting. The confidence I had in the project started fading and in the middle of trying to force it forward, I stopped.

I remembered what I had already committed to: Asking God to order my steps.

That's not just something I say. I literally have it tattooed on me.

Yes—another tattoo, but this time, it's on my foot.

That wasn't just ink. It was instruction. If I really believed my steps were being ordered, I had to stop dragging my feet when the direction was "no."

This wasn't the first time I had to ask God to step in and lead. I've done it in relationships, too. I've asked Him, "If this isn't for me, show me or shut it down," and He always does what's best for me.

Even though this was business, financial increase, I had to listen.

Letting go of that launch allowed me to reclaim my alignment without losing momentum. What I built next came from a clearer place, with stronger support and more intentional leadership.

Obedience is the strategy.

Peace and clarity are the signs.

The most successful thing you can do is to sit in it until your conviction is undeniable.

CHAPTER SIX

THE ART OF COURSE-CORRECTING

Now, we couldn't walk you through all this transformation without addressing the art, or should we say, the courage of course-correcting.

This is the kind of shift that asks you to release what you once prayed for. The kind that makes you second-guess your own decisions because this was the vision. This was the partnership. This business was your baby and now, you're choosing to step away from it.

The art of course-correcting means making the hard, necessary pivot when the path no longer reflects your purpose.

Let me be clear, there is difference between quitting and course- correcting. Quitting is rooted in avoidance. Course-correction is rooted in awareness.

Course-correction asks that you look at something and say: "This isn't working." It's no longer aligned, honest, nor a reflection of where I'm going next.

Maybe it's a product you launched that's no longer selling or a program that's draining your energy more than it's delivering results. Think about a brand that doesn't even feel or sound like you anymore. Whatever it is, you've outgrown it and staying in it just because it once worked is no longer a good enough reason.

Listen: You don't owe your past self an apology for evolving. You owe your future self the truth, and the truth is, the most strategic step to take is to stop. Stop forcing it. Stop trying to make it make sense. Stop building on a blueprint that wasn't designed for the version of you that exists now.

Entrepreneurship will have you mastering things that no longer match your mission. You'll get good at the wrong things just to keep up with what others claim is successful. Leading the type of company that you never actually wanted.

Then, you'll wake up one day and realize the thing you've been maintaining is the very thing keeping you stuck. Whether it's a bad deal you signed without enough due diligence, employees you've kept on payroll because they're friends with talent or family with history, even though you know they don't have the skills or drive to take the business where you're headed. You have structure, systems, and a strategy that you've clearly outgrown but feel guilty changing.

This is where courage collides with truth and both will cost you. Course-correcting always does.

It costs you comfort. It costs you applause. It might even cost you loyal customers who loved the old version (and prices) of you.

But what you gain? Alignment. Capacity. Sustainability.

The opportunity to change direction with intention and without second-guessing your growth. Trust that if something is no longer serving you, it's costing more than it's contributing.

YOUR TURN

What plan have you committed to that no longer reflects your current capacity or goals?

_____
_____
_____
_____
_____
_____
_____

What warning signs have you brushed off because you didn't want to "start over"?

_____
_____
_____
_____
_____
_____
_____

Where are you trying to sustain a pace or structure that's already draining you?

_____
_____
_____
_____
_____
_____
_____

If you scaled back with intention, not fear, what could actually improve?

_____
_____
_____
_____
_____
_____

Take inventory of what's still serving you and what isn't. Then adjust accordingly.

CLARITY REWIRED: THE COURSE-CORRECTION SCAN

Before pushing forward on a plan, run it through this filter:

1. **Am I excited—or just exhausted?**
   If you're dragging yourself through the process, something's misaligned. Excitement doesn't mean it's easy. But it shouldn't feel like dread.

2. **Am I building from clarity—or from pressure?**
   Don't create just to meet an expectation. Build from conviction, not obligation.

3. **Is this the vision—or just the version I thought would work?**
   In some cases, the plan needs to change. That's not quitting. That's maturing.

If the answer feels muddy, pause and adjust. Better to shift early than to launch something you already resent.

REWIRED IN REAL LIFE

Shannon has been a long-term retainer client of mine. She's steady, sharp, and typically ahead of the curve. During one of our most ambitious projects together, she was planning her most elevated event yet: a multi-day, multi-destination adventure retreat designed for those craving both escape and expansion.

It wasn't just big, it was public. Over 2,000 RSVPs had already rolled in. Speakers were confirmed, vendors booked, the experience fully branded and broadcast across her platforms.

But five weeks out, the wheels started to shake.

Behind the viral content and epic design, her internal team was exhausted. Details were slipping. Deadlines were being missed. Shannon, usually composed and confident, was known for her poker face, but this time, her lack of enthusiasm was obvious. She wasn't excited anymore. She was carrying the whole thing like a burden rather than an experience carefully crafted to push attendees out of their routine and into the unforgettable.

We pulled back and looked at the facts.

We started with self-assessment.

What was actually happening beneath the surface? We didn't gloss over the exhaustion or label it "just stress." We examined the build. The venues were complex. The structure demanded nonstop energy. Her team didn't have the event experience to manage a retreat at this scale without burning out. Shannon's event planner had designed a schedule that left zero margin for rest, recovery, or flexibility.

Then came effective communication.

Shannon had to lead direct conversations with her team, her sponsors, and her guest speakers. She wasn't offering explanations. She owned the moment, and because there was communication with transparency, the respect didn't decrease. It deepened.

Next, we applied forecasting.

What would happen if she kept pushing forward at the current pace? Best-case: the event would happen, but the team would fracture. Worst-case: the quality would suffer, and the long-term damage to her brand and reputation could take months or even years to repair. We mapped the financial, emotional, and operational costs, then dealt with them directly.

Finally, we committed to consistent change.

We adjusted the framework, but not the foundation. The schedule was trimmed. Sessions were restructured. We secured new venues that offered stronger support and greater flexibility. The focus transitioned from large-scale production to facilitated excursions, reflective challenges, high-energy gatherings, and transformational moments.

Every external update reflected the brand's values and modeled steady leadership without losing control or spinning our wheels.

The outcome?

The event didn't just sell out, it exceeded every benchmark we'd set. The energy was unmatched, the feedback undeniable. Shannon walked away not just with momentum, but with a renewed sense of direction and a model she could scale with confidence.

That's the real art of course-correcting.

Strategic decisions that protect the vision and the person pursuing it.

CHAPTER SEVEN

WHEN YOU OUTGROW THE ROOM

Nobody talks about what it feels like to outgrow a room.

We talk about being the underdog and earning our seat at the table. But we don't talk enough about the moment you look around and realize: I don't belong here anymore. I've grown so far beyond this.

There is the friend group where the conversations have not matured and their lifestyles no longer align with your priorities. Your future is being held hostage by an outdated goal that once felt like the dream and now you finally achieved it and it didn't look or feel the way you thought it would.

If you're here, trust me, you're not being ungrateful, you're being honest. That version of the dream no longer satisfies you.

It's an uncomfortable space, because it's not always toxic. It can be familiar, filled with people you love and have built with from the beginning. Remaining in a version of your life that no longer reflects your values, vision, or voice is not growth; it is stagnation. Sometimes what you have outgrown is not a place or a relationship. It is the shallow version of who you used to be. This is the version that played small, built quickly without depth, said yes to everything, acted on impulse, and found identity in performance.

At this point in your growth, you've matured past the hustle mindset and you've started living from a place of vision rather than validation. The focus and confidence you've gained is shifting the way you live, how you build, and how you lead.

As this internal shift deepens, old roles start to feel restrictive. What once felt like alignment now feels like resistance. That's when it hits you, the room didn't change—but you did!

My oh the ache of expansion.

Here you find yourself frustrated because you're doing the work. You're rewiring, applying the principles, and growing. Unfortunately, you've also outpaced the mentors who once stretched you. The title, the identity, the pace you used to keep, it all feels like it's lacking because your current story is outgrowing the old story you once told yourself about who you needed to be.

So, you pause. You reflect. You listen to the quiet pull toward something bigger. You can feel it, subtle, but steady.

The sense that you are being called to do more. Staying in a place you have outgrown will not just delay your next level. It will drain you in the process.

Growth demands this level of awareness and awareness is only powerful when you act on it.

I've walked away from spaces that were once the most valuable to my being, but they no longer supported who I was becoming. My advice to you is that when you feel that nudge, it's not your job to explain it away. It's your job to acknowledge it.

Ask yourself:
1. What space am I still holding onto out of habit, not purpose?

2. What part of me is showing up for a version of success that I've already outgrown?

3. What have I stayed loyal to simply because I was afraid to pivot?

Leaving this way of life behind means you've recognized that where you're going next can't be built in a comfort zone that you've already mastered.

Growth often comes disguised. It shows up as fatigue, disinterest, agitation, and the slow awareness of the widening and undeniable gap between what you are capable of and what your surroundings still expect of you.

There's no need to plan a grand exit. You don't have to explain your growth or justify your evolution. You simply need to make a grounded decision rooted in who you are now. Let your next decision reflect your future, not your past. The room served its purpose. Now it's time to step into the assignment your growth has made room for.

YOUR TURN

What have you outgrown that you're still managing out of loyalty or fear?

_____
_____
_____
_____
_____
_____
_____

What roles or routines are you holding onto out of obligation, not alignment?

_____
_____
_____
_____
_____
_____
_____

What space would you step into if you weren't worried about how others might react?

_____
_____
_____
_____
_____
_____
_____

Who still expects the old version of you and how have you been performing to meet that expectation?

_____
_____
_____
_____
_____
_____
_____

What would trusting your evolution actually look like this week?

_____
_____
_____
_____
_____
_____
_____

Don't confuse loyalty with limitation. Growth doesn't make you disloyal. It makes you ready.

CLARITY REWIRED

Use this when you know you've outgrown something but need help moving forward with purpose:

1. What environment, circle, or commitment no longer matches the vision I have for my next level and what's one boundary I can set this week to honor that?

2. What new space or opportunity has already started to present itself, and how can I begin preparing to enter it?

3. What decision have I been postponing because I'm afraid of being misunderstood and what would it look like if I chose growth over approval?

Let this be your reminder: you don't have to stay where you've been just because it's familiar. You get to choose from alignment now.

REWIRED IN REAL LIFE

My client Nathan inherited a business from his parents. A small, respected operation that had served the local Filipino community for decades. In their culture, family legacy was sacred. Stability was the goal, and change felt like disrespect to those who built the business with their bare hands.

Transitioning him into ownership required more than navigating business strategy. He was up against generational expectations, family and emotional ties, alongside a cultural norm that said: "If it's not broken, don't fix it."

Here's the thing, Nathan had a vision that stretched beyond tradition. He saw what the company *could* be: a streamlined backend, expanded digital presence, AI-driven customer experience, and more scalable offerings.

Still, every time he tried to innovate, his parents reminded him, "This is how we've done it for 37 years. Why change now?"

I'll never forget one of our sessions. He lowered his head, so defeated, fighting back the tears welling up in his eyes, and said the saddest thing: "I'm not trying to disrespect their legacy. I'm trying to make sure it doesn't get left behind."

So, we worked together to honor the mission while modernizing the model. Slowly, we integrated automation, revamped the service flow, and updated their brand.

We got caught having a good laugh imagining the business still running on laminated paper files. His parents side-eyed us like every new tech tool was intended to scam them.

His parents eventually recognized their son was true to his word. He didn't erase their legacy. He just expanded it.

Outgrowing the room doesn't mean tearing it down. It means redesigning it to fit the version of you who's leading now.

PHASE III
THE EXPANSION

FOCUS:

EXECUTION

VISIBILITY

SCALABILITY

CHAPTER EIGHT
CEO ENERGY

Anyone can add "CEO" to their bio. Few lead with vision, delegate with discernment, and make decisions that serve the future instead of reacting to the fire right in front of them.

Being a founder means you started the journey. Being a C.E.O requires that you know how to sustain it.

The difference lies in energy and not the trendy buzzword kind, but the kind that shows up in how you prioritize, prepare, and protect what you're building. You can't fake that.

It shows up in the way you run meetings, support your team, manage your money, make hard decisions, and uphold standards most avoid.

CEO energy is built on quiet strength. No titles. No talking. Just consistency and anchored leadership.

Clear leadership drives successful, sustainable and profitable growth.

Consistency behind the scenes matters more than visibility online. The discipline to persevere when no one is watching, the structure that holds even when motivation fades, and the focus to follow through when no one is clapping is essential. Authority doesn't have to be proven, but it for sure needs to be trusted. That trust is built through strategy, execution, and through decisions that align with a bigger vision.

CEO energy can't suddenly appear once the money comes in or the team is built. It has to lead the way. Your energy has to set the tone and if you have scattered energy, it will create scattered direction. Reactivity will create fragile systems. When systems are missing, chaos fills the gap.

A business can only rise to the level of the person leading it. If you do not evolve, neither will it.

That is why renovation is required.

WHEN RENOVATION IS REQUIRED

You've heard the saying, *"Don't throw the baby out with the bathwater."*

That's sound advice, until the bathwater is moldy, the tub is cracked, and the plumbing hasn't worked in years.

At that point, a deep clean won't cut it. The entire house needs to be stripped down and rebuilt from the studs up.

This renovation is preparing you to build with longevity in mind and create an infrastructure that reflects with scale and substance as the new vision.

I once heard my mentor's mentor describe what they evaluate during business acquisitions. It stuck with me. They assess five critical areas: People, Structure, Systems, Strategy, and Execution. That means all cards on the table.

There are scenarios when leadership must be reassessed. The team that helped you launch and grow may no longer have the capacity or creativity to thrive at the next level. Your startup strategy is most likely already outdated. The structure that held you together may now be limiting your expansion. Even execution, once your strength, can become a bottleneck when you are no longer the right person to manage certain areas of the business.

Renovation is a form of discipline. Be willing to take inventory of what still works, what holds you back, and what needs to be reimagined, even if you built it from scratch. If it once represented your best, then it's time to raise the bar.

There's no need to tear anything down just to destroy it. Rebuild to support growth.

What once was the ceiling can now serve as the floor.

YOUR TURN

Where are you leading like a founder, but being required to lead like a CEO?

_____
_____
_____
_____
_____
_____
_____

What systems or habits still reflect your starting point, not your current capacity?

_____
_____
_____
_____
_____
_____
_____

Where does your energy need to become more focused and less frantic?

_____
_____
_____
_____
_____
_____
_____

What area of your life are you avoiding because of how much change it will require?

_____
_____
_____
_____
_____
_____
_____

Audit it. Then lead like the energy you bring sets the standard.

CLARITY REWIRED

Use this section when your leadership feels heavy or your business feels stuck in place.

1. What decision would a clear, confident CEO make at this exact moment?

2. Which area of my business needs leadership—not just effort?

3. If I were hiring someone else to lead this business, what would I expect them to clean up or rebuild right away?

4. What role does my energy play in what's thriving—and what's failing?

Make decisions from the seat you're growing into, not the one you're trying to maintain.

REWIRED IN REAL LIFE

Embarking on the entrepreneurial journey as a woman brings a unique set of challenges and insights.

Don't worry, this one's still for the fellas too.

While the path may look different depending on who's walking it, the lessons in leadership, growth, and building to last are universal.

Reflecting on my own path, there are pivotal lessons I wish I had embraced from the start. I want to share them with you to cut your learning curve.

1. Embrace Imperfection and Delegate

The pursuit of perfection can be paralyzing. In my early entrepreneurial years, I believed I needed to master every aspect of my business. I wore every hat, held every role, and ran myself into the ground and quickly became exhausted and inefficient. Over time, I realized the power of focusing on my strengths and entrusting other talented professionals to shine in their zone of genius so I could lead in mine.

2. Your Perspective Is the Advantage

For a long time, I tried to sound like "them." I'd water down my approach, soften my voice, or over-explain just to be taken seriously in rooms that weren't built with me in mind. What I've learned? Your distinct perspective, the way you lead, your lived experience, those aren't things to hide.

They're your edge. The marketplace doesn't need more duplicates. It needs real people bringing real solutions in real time.

3. Build With Range; Diversity Matters

In the beginning, I leaned too heavily on people who looked like me, thought like me, and worked the same way I did. It felt familiar, but familiar isn't what builds scale. I had to intentionally seek out people who challenged my assumptions, stretched my systems, and better reflected the diverse clientele we served. That's where growth happens.

4. Trust Your Gut, Even the Subtle Signs

Everybody has an opinion. In business, they're usually not shy about sharing it. In the noise, I used to second-guess what I knew to be true. I'd override it with logic, strategy, or someone else's opinion. Listen, your gut will rarely scream at you. It's a whisper, a quiet tension, a "something ain't right!" Pay attention to that. Learning to trust my instincts and discern which advice aligned with my mission was instrumental.

5. Failure Isn't Fatal

Failure has been one of my best teachers. It forced me to slow down, revisit my strategy and cut the fat. Every time something fell apart, I learned how to build it better.

I stopped framing it as proof that I wasn't ready and started treating it like the training ground for lessons in execution, timing, leadership, stewardship, and resilience.

CEO ENERGY BONUS: ARCHITECT OF THE VISION

These aren't just inspirational one-liners that come from a podcast or a panel; they're truths I earned. If you're serious about building to last, you'll earn your own too. These come from diving in head first for the experience. Try, fail, lead, and learn in real time.

Whether you're just getting started or you've been at this for years, remember: you don't have to get it perfect. You just have to keep growing into the leader your business actually needs.

That's how you bring CEO Energy.

Don't just put your name on the door, build with a vision that outlasts ego, outgrows trends, and outperforms itself year after year.

You're not here to play the part; you're here to architect the vision. Future-focused and results-driven. One built with intention, reinforced by structure, and carried out through consistent execution.

The integrity of your foundation determines how far it can go, so move with purpose. Execute with precision. Reinvision what's possible and then build it.

Now you're a CEO in motion.

CHAPTER NINE

REWIRED BY DESIGN

I asked one of my mentors a question during a live Q & A session:

"If you had to start from scratch with zero dollars and zero resources but you still had all the knowledge you have now, what would you do?"

He skipped the motivation and went straight to execution. No hype. Just tactical steps.

He'd go back to work. Iron work. Long hours, hard labor. He'd sleep on an air mattress. Stack sixty thousand in a year. Stay disciplined. Then he'd start with just one option contract in the stock market. He'd invest wisely. Build back slowly. Launch a YouTube channel. Teach people how to build while working. Sell digital products. Speak to audiences. Help others out of their nine-to-five while rebuilding himself, step by step.

No shortcuts. No shame. No ego.

Intention, alignment, and design.

That's the purpose of this chapter.

To remind you that you need a blueprint and architected growth.

After everything you've rewired up to this point, the greatest risk is unintentionally recreating the very model that left you burnt out, misaligned, or trapped in chaos.

This is the turning point. No more building around convenience, crisis, or the expectations of others. From here, you build with strategy, conviction, and values you actually live by. Never again will you build a business that simply functions. You build one that's designed to sustain. Scalable, strategic and soul-aligned. Built for the future and grounded in what actually drives you, because your next level of success demands more than vision. It demands design.

DESIGN PRINCIPLES THAT MATTER NOW

The world is changing fast and it's only getting faster.

Visibility is noisy. Trust is low. Buyers are more skeptical than ever and yet, there is a wide-open lane for business owners who set themselves apart with substance, discernment, and strategic conviction.

That's where creative development becomes a competitive edge.

Every element of how you design shapes the business and the builder.

Here are the principles that should be guiding your next evolution:

1. **Vision**
   Where are you actually going? What does success look and feel like, beyond income goals and vanity metrics? A business with no vision is just a job on autopilot.

2. **Values**
   What non-negotiables guide your decisions? Are you building for power, impact, legacy, or lifestyle? Get certain, or you'll chase someone else's dream by default.

3. **Voice**
   What do you stand for, and how does that show up in

your branding, your leadership, and your delivery? If you disappear from the feed, would your audience feel it?

4. **Viability**
   Does the model make sense today and three years from now? Do the margins support growth, or are you scaling burnout? Does the infrastructure reflect where you're headed?

Design = Direction.

THE GAP BETWEEN VISION AND EXECUTION

Having vision is usually not the problem. Most entrepreneurs are full of ideas. We can talk about where we want our company to go, what kind of freedom we want to create, what impact we want to make.

There's a gap that's not found in the dreaming. It's found in the design.

Here's what happens in the wild:

We sketch out a big vision but never restructure the business model to support it. We talk about financial freedom but keep pricing like we're in survival. We say we want to scale but are still operating from the hustler's roadmap. We keep striving for "more" without ever defining what meaningful looks like.

Then here's the amen or ouch moment, when we say we want to build impact, when what we really mean is—we want to feel significant.

That's why vision alone isn't enough.

Design is what closes the gap.

We get tested in the process. Our discipline will show in the margins. CEO energy shows up in how we make vision executable without losing the values that sparked it.

Systems, decisions, and structures that flex and evolve is how you truly get Rewired by design.

THE WHITEBOARD REWIRED

Use this section as your strategic blueprint. The same way you'd step into a business planning retreat—only this time, you're not waiting on a facilitator. You are the one leading.

Grab a whiteboard, a notebook, or a quiet room. No distractions.

Let this session shape your next chapter in full "make ish happen" mode.

1. **What problem do I still care about solving—even if the business model changes?** Strip away the format, the products, the delivery. What impact do you still want to have?

2. **What have I built that no longer reflects who I am or how I work best?** Be honest. If you didn't already own it, would you start it again today?

3. **What parts of my current business model feel like a performance?** Where are you still trying to prove something or please someone?

4. **What would I immediately remove if fear or judgment weren't in the equation?** What are you clinging to because it's familiar—not because it's fruitful?

5. **If this business disappeared tomorrow, what would I rebuild—and what would I leave behind?** This is honesty in its purest form.

6. **What must be true for my next version of growth to feel aligned, powerful, and worth it?** Think infrastructure, team, pricing, visibility, time, and energy.

Your mindset is rewired. You've redefined how you show up for yourself and in your business.

Now comes the choice:

Will you keep repeating cycles disguised as growth? Or will you commit to building differently this time?

Draft your blueprint deliberately, intelligently, and on your own terms.

The next chapter isn't waiting, it's already unfolding. Design it like you mean it.

REWIRED IN REAL LIFE: NEXTFLIX REIMAGINED

Before Netflix became a household name for streaming, it was a DVD-by-mail service competing with Blockbuster, an industry giant at the time. Customers would log into their account, select the movies they wanted, and wait for them to arrive in the mail. It was innovative... but only for a moment. The world was changing rapidly.

Internet speed was improving, slowly but surely. People were spending more time on their computers than ever before. Broadband was starting to replace dial-up. YouTube was exploding in popularity. Smartphones hadn't fully taken over yet, but digital consumption was climbing across the board.

We were entering a new era and you could feel it.
People weren't just watching content anymore. They were multitasking, skipping commercials, and expecting instant access. The patience for slow, clunky processes was wearing thin. The convenience economy had arrived and companies that didn't adjust would get left behind.

Netflix paid attention.

Instead of getting comfortable with what was working in the moment, their leadership team made a bold decision: they would start designing for the future.

They knew streaming was coming, even though the infrastructure wasn't fully there yet. The average household didn't have lightning-speed internet just yet and most people were still renting DVDs on weekends.

Netflix saw what others ignored: convenience always wins. People wanted what they wanted, when they wanted it and streaming would eventually offer just that.

So they reimagined the business.

They redistributed resources away from their proven DVD rental model and began building what would become their streaming platform. It wasn't an overnight transition. In fact, they ran both models in parallel for years. They made small, intentional moves, investing in tech, testing user behavior, building licensing deals, until the streaming side wasn't just an add-on. It *was* the business.

And then they did it again.

Once streaming became the norm, Netflix realized that licensing shows from other studios gave them visibility but not ownership. So they moved into producing original content. Not because they were ready, but because they knew staying ready meant building control over their next chapter.

Producing shows wasn't in their wheelhouse. They weren't a Hollywood studio. They were a tech company. But they knew if they wanted long-term control and brand authority, they needed to own the IP (intellectual property). So they greenlit shows like *House of Cards* and *Orange Is the New Black* and the market responded.

Viewers didn't just watch. They binged. They canceled their cable subscriptions. They stopped waiting for network television to tell them what to like and just like that, Netflix went from "that DVD company" to *the* cultural curator of a generation.

None of that happened by accident.

They rewired with vision, values, and bold execution.

They didn't wait until they were losing money or becoming irrelevant. They started while things were still working. That's what strategic design looks like. You can't just scale, you must evolve... Thoughtfully. Proactively. Intentionally. That's what you're being called to do.

Don't course-correct when forced. Design a business that can stand and be consistent in change, rise with innovation, and serve people better than anyone else in your industry.

When you build by design, you don't just respond to the market, you shape it.

CHAPTER TEN

WHAT'S NEXT

My hope is that this was more than just a journey through another self-help /business book. It was a reset. A deeper return to the parts of you that needed to be challenged, stretched, and redefined. You peeled back the layers in how you think, decide, and lead in business.

Along the way, you stripped away the foundation that was built on old survival tactics and replaced it with structure that reflects how you think, work, and win now. You faced hard truths and owned them without excuses. You stopped looking for quick fixes and started making strategic, aligned decisions.

With new standards for how you operate, your CEO energy has evolved, quietly, steadily, and without any need for external validation.

From here, your growth stops being a conversation and becomes a commitment.

You're no longer just in motion, you're in position!

THE CHALLENGE

So here's the final challenge:

Before you turn this last page and go back to the scroll, or the job, or the business —

Take one step.

Take one action that reflects everything you've realigned:
- Send the email that was due 2 days ago.
- Schedule the meeting that you know could open the door to your next opportunity.
- Rewrite the offer because you're no longer decreasing your value (or revenue).
- Cancel the thing that you really didn't want to go to anyway.
- Launch the ugly version. (Shoutout to the **Do It Ugly** brand.)
- Go to bed at 11 like you've been promising yourself for a month.
- Call your mama like you've been saying you need to all week.

Start the thing - just the first step.

WHAT'S NEXT

Finish the thing - because it's actually already done but just needs (fill in the blank.)

Release the fear because it's not doing you any favors.

You're more than capable of it. You've proven that. Now let your next step reflect it.

FROM INSIGHTS TO EXECUTION

You know how to do hard things. You've already done them.

Consistent action that aligns with your values is the prerequisite for your next chapter.

You were never meant to play small; proceed with confidence.

YOUR TURN: THE REWIRED VERSION

What's one decision you've been delaying that you're ready to make today with no turning back?

_____
_____
_____
_____
_____
_____

Where will you show up differently now that clarity is no longer the issue?

_____
_____
_____
_____
_____
_____

What system or structure are you committed to building in the next 30 days to support your next level?

_____
_____
_____
_____
_____
_____
_____

What part of your vision are you no longer holding back or negotiating with?

_____
_____
_____
_____
_____
_____
_____
_____

REWIRED IN REAL LIFE: WHEN THE WORK STICKS

I once heard someone say people aren't afraid of failure, they're afraid of success. For a long time, I thought it was just a clever quote. But then I started listening. Really listening...to the entrepreneurs who had systems, strategy, and support, but still hadn't launched.

I had a client who was profiting $2M a year and still questioning if they're doing enough.

Then there were clients with full teams who still triple-checked everything before handing off a task.

I saw imposter syndrome and the need for control. Sometimes it was about proving their worth to people who stopped watching a long time ago and other times they didn't know who they were outside of the struggle.

Success demands "different" from you.

This is your moment.

This is the shift.

This is Business Rewired™.

FINAL ACKNOWLEDGMENTS

Every page, every story, every lesson is the result of real moments. Some filled with breakthroughs, others filled with heartbreak. This wasn't a book of theory. This was *me,* walking through leadership, life, entrepreneurship, and everything in between.

To You, the Reader—Thank you for doing the hard thing.

For picking up this book not just to feel inspired, but to actually be *different* on the other side of it. Thank you for letting me speak into the parts of you that you don't always share out loud.

For trusting these pages enough to wrestle with truth and show up for yourself, your vision, and your future.

I don't take that lightly. I believe in you.

To Alexis—My business bestie—you've been the push, the mirror, the reminder to keep going. Thank you for being in every room with me whether physically or spiritually. Now let's go get what's ours.

To Ednethia—God always connects us at just the right time for the next level of purpose. The type of sister chemistry that couldn't have been created by force, it had to be divinely orchestrated.

To Dr. Sue Carter-Collins—Thank you for being a spiritual compass and a trusted voice in my journey. Your wisdom continues to help me navigate entrepreneurship without ever losing sight of what matters most. I always strive to keep God at the center of how I operate, and your guidance makes sure that never wavers.

To Leon, Wallstreet Trapper—Your example as a business owner has been more than instrumental, it's been foundational. Watching you navigate with authenticity, and unapologetic purpose taught me what it means to move with bold conviction. #**GOD & Money.**

To Jose—thank you for speaking my name in rooms I'm not in yet. Your belief in me reminds me of what's possible when someone sees the vision, even when it's still becoming clear.

Connect With Me!

If this book moved you, challenged you, or inspired you, don't stop here.

Whether you're looking to rewire your mindset, your systems, or your next business move, I'd love to support you on the journey.

→ **Visit YourBusinessRewired.com** to learn more, connect with my team, and explore tools, resources, and strategy sessions tailored to where you are and where you're headed.

Use the QR code below to book a free strategy call.

We'll be here when you're ready to move from *potential* to *power*.

www.ingramcontent.com/pod-product-compliance
Lightning Source LLC
Chambersburg PA
CBHW030222170426
43194CB00007BA/831